Get Around

in the City

by Lee Sullivan Hill

NATIONAL GEOGRAPHIC

Hampton-Brown

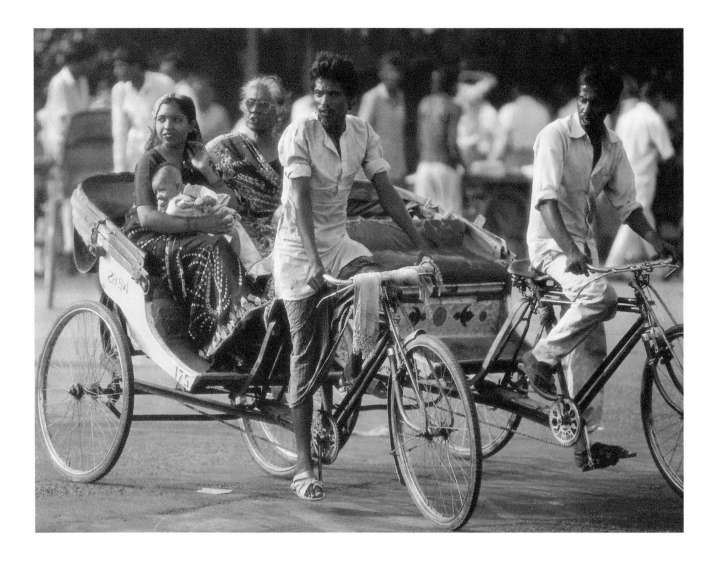

Zoom-zoom, beep-beep. Get around in the city. Transportation takes you where you want to go.

In a city full of people, there are many ways to get around. There are big cars, small cars, old and new. There are taxicabs and trucks and vans. What a traffic jam!

Get around on foot. You might get there faster. City buildings are close together. You can walk from store to store.

Some streets are closed to cars and open to people. Crowds of walkers flow like rivers.

Crowds of bike riders get around, too. Some cities have roadways just for bikes.

Some kinds of transportation are made to share. Buses roll from stop to stop. You can catch a bus to get uptown.

Climb the steep stairs of a double-decker bus. The world looks different from way up there.

You can get around a big city on a train. Trains move from stop to stop on rails.

In San Francisco, cable cars ride
on rails in the middle of the street.
Underground cables move the cars
up and and down steep hills.

In cities near the water, you can get around by boat. Ferryboats in New York City carry groups of people across the water.

Everyone uses boats in Venice, Italy. The city was built on islands. Taxi boats and gondolas glide up and down canals.

People in some cities use animals for transportation. How would you like to get around on an elephant?

Some city workers must get around FAST! Firefighters in shiny engines rush to a fire.

Police cards zoom to the rescue.
Sirens blare, lights flash.
Everyone get out of the way!

Other people like to slow down and look around. Clip-clop down a stone street. It doesn't matter where you go. The fun part is the ride.

How would you choose to get around in the city? Going on a field trip? Take a school bus.

In a hurry? Grab a cab.

On a sunny day, you might want to walk.

If it's raining, try the subway.
It goes underground.

In cities around the world, people find all kinds of ways to get around.

Day or night, the city
never stops moving.

Photo Index

Cover The Metromover carries passengers high above the crowds of Miami, Florida. It is called a monorail because it runs on a single rail. (*Mono* in *monorail* means "one.")

Page 2 Rickshaw drivers in Bombay, India, pedal paying passengers all over the city. Rickshaws take the place of taxicabs in many cities. They look like big tricycles.

Page 3 About 14,000,000 people live in Beijing, China, where this photo was taken. From Beijing to Boston, traffic jams are part of city life.

Page 4 This photo of New York City shows an amazing variety of vehicles. Taxicabs carry passengers, cars weave through the traffic, and trucks and vans pick up and deliver goods.

Page 5 People enjoy strolling down High Street in Kilkenny, Ireland. With its shops, restaurants, and wide sidewalks, Kilkenny is friendly to pedestrians.

Page 6 This photo of a crowded street was taken on a Sunday afternoon in Beijing, China. A street set aside for walkers is called a pedestrian mall.

Page 7 Bicycles and cars are separated from each other on this road in Chengdu, China. Barricades keep bicyclists safe from motor vehicles.

Page 8 A bus makes its way through traffic in Panama City, Panama. Buses, trains, trolleys, subways, and ferryboats are a few kinds of shared public transportation.

Page 9 People who live in London, England, ride red double-decker buses to offices and shops and back home again. Tourists ride them just for fun. Narrow steps curve up to the top level of each bus.

Page 10 The El train in Chicago, Illinois, got its name from the word *elevated*. The tracks are raised high above the ground. People, cars, trucks, and buses can move underneath.

Page 11 Even though the cable cars of San Francisco, California, are old, residents keep them running. The cable cars have become a symbol of the city.

Page 12 Millions of people travel across New York Harbor every year on the Staten Island Ferry. Most are commuters, who ride each day to jobs in Manhattan.

Page 13 The Grand Canal is one of the main waterways in Venice, Italy. It is so wide that hundreds of boats can gather there.

Page 14 Elephants are highly valued in Southeast Asia for their great strength. In Jaipur, India, they give rides to tourists. Outside the city, elephants carry cargo, haul lumber, and carve roads through the forest.

Page 15 This aerial ladder truck is operated by firefighters in San Francisco, California. It takes two drivers to steer the long truck around corners. One driver sits in front and the other sits in back.

Page 16 The New York City Police Department, like most others, uses cars that have been fixed up to help officers do their jobs. The cars have heavy-duty shock absorbers, sirens and lights, and even laptop computers.

Page 17 This horse-drawn carriage in Quebec City, Canada, might make you imagine the olden days. Before cars were invented, horses were a major form of transportation.

Page 18 This school bus in San Juan, Puerto Rico, is picking up students after a field trip to Old San Juan.

Page 19 These taxicabs are driving through Times Square in New York City. A cab can zip you right to the front door of a Broadway theater to see a show.

Page 20 This woman walks through her neighborhood in Bhaktapur, Nepal. Walking is the oldest form of transportation, and it's still one of the best ways to get around in the city.

Page 21 This subway train runs underground in Santiago, Chile. Subway riders avoid bad weather and heavy traffic on city streets.

Page 22 A donkey pulls a homemade cart in Alma-Ata, Kazakhstan. People make use of whatever kind of transportation they can find to get around in the city.

Page 23 Nighttime traffic rolls along Michigan Avenue, while lights glitter and glow on the stone walls of the Old Water Tower in Chicago, Illinois.